from us all at
Shutelake.

Glorious DEVON

Described by Reginald J. W. Hammond
with Foreword by S. P. B. Mais.

Painted by H. Sutton Palmer R.I.,
Henry B. Wimbush and other artists

SALMON

Published by
J Salmon Limited
100 London Road, Sevenoaks,
Kent TN13 1BB

First edition 1995
Designed by the Salmon Studio

ISBN 1 898435 41 3

Printed in England by
J Salmon Limited, Tubs Hill Works
Sevenoaks, Kent

BY BIDEFORD BRIDGE

Coloured Illustrations

A DEVON COTTAGE AT BERRYNARBOR

FOREWORD

DEVON IS BY FAR the loveliest of all the English counties. Its soil is a rich terra-cotta, as red as its famous cattle, and its many rivers, with their sources on the peat moors, glow like mahogany. The valleys through which these rivers run are bordered by thickly wooded combes and lush green pastures. The cottages in the hamlets and villages are in the main thatched, white with stucco walls; roses, fuchsias and hydrangeas flourish in abundance in colourful gardens.

The coasts of North and South Devon could scarcely be more different. The South Coast boasts many splendid, sheltered, sandy beaches, protected from all winds except the South. The North Coast is much more open, severe and rugged, with high sea cliffs and little protection against the Atlantic gales and also has wide sandy beaches at Woolacombe and Saunton.

A large area of North Devon is occupied by the forest of Exmoor; rolling, undulating moorland of heather and bracken and the haunt of red deer. Far wilder and much larger is Dartmoor, in South Devon; two hundred square miles of trackless land with many curious shaped tors of granite rearing up out of the moor. At the very top of this tree-less wilderness are the sources of the famous Devon rivers, Taw, Teign, Dart, Tavy and Okement, whilst to the south is a well-wooded, soft and gentle country.

The delights of the county are the many high-banked hedges made of earth and stone, smothered in ferns and wild flowers and the rich countryside cut into squares of yellow and green and red, in which the red soil always predominates; a land of orchards and opulent pastures.

AN OLD CORNER, BRIXHAM

Sidmouth

SOUTH DEVON

The long southern coastline of South Devon is famous for its rich red sandstone cliffs. They stretch from Sidmouth to Torbay and beyond and are intersected by creeks and estuaries. At one such break in the line is Sidmouth, a popular resort at the mouth of the little River Sid. A pebble and shingle beach is sheltered by Peak Hill on the west and Salcombe Hill on the east.

Eastward lie the little villages of Branscombe and Beer with the towering Beer Head, 400 feet of chalk rock, between. Beyond Beer lies Seaton, a quiet resort with sand and shingle beach at the mouth of the River Axe.

Inland from Sidmouth is Ottery St. Mary famous for its beautiful fourteenth century collegiate church. A little further north is the fine Tudor manor house of Cadhay. To the west of the mouth of the River Otter lies Budleigh Salterton where there is pleasant bathing

COTTAGES AT BRANSCOMBE

BLOSSOM TIME AT AXMOUTH

THE EXE AT TOPSHAM

EXETER FROM THE CANAL

from a pebble beach. Two miles inland is East Budleigh, an attractive village of thatched cottages. The old church has some notable carved bench-ends. At nearby Hayes Barton is the farmhouse where Sir Walter Raleigh was born in 1552. Nearby too are the beautiful Bicton Gardens.

The Guildhall, Exeter

Exmouth is a popular resort on the east bank of the Exe estuary across which a ferry connects with Starcross. There are fine sands, sports and entertainments. Enjoyable walks may be taken to Littleham and to the pretty riverside village of Lympstone where is A-La-Ronde, a curious circular house built in 1798 with a shell gallery and a collection of prints.

The ancient city of Exeter, Devon's busy county town, lies on the River Exe nine miles from its mouth. There are good shops and a market, and plenty of entertainment. The imposing Guildhall, with its beautiful Elizabethan portico jutting over the pavement in High Street, is one of the oldest municipal buildings in England. The famous Cathedral with its exquisite West Front is principally of the Decorated style but retains its two massive Norman towers. The Lady Chapel occupies

THE SOUTH TOWER, EXETER CATHEDRAL

WIDECOMBE-IN-THE-MOOR

the site of the original Saxon monastic church. Of great interest is the fourteenth century astronomical clock. The Bishop's Palace containing a valuable library stands in lovely grounds. In the Close is the charming Elizabethan Mol's Coffee House. The remnants of Rougement Castle, built by William the Conqueror, stand in the gardens near the railway station.

Bickleigh village lies on the east bank of the Exe eight miles north of Exeter. A Saxon chapel here has a thatched roof and the re-

The Bridges at Dartmeet

maining parts of an old castle include a Norman doorway. A little to the south-west is the Iron Age earthwork of Cadbury Castle, a wonderful viewpoint. Pleasantly situated in the Exe valley to the north lies Tiverton, notable for the Greenway Chapel in St. Peter's Church, the old castle gateway and Blundell's School.

South-west of Exeter is the 360 square mile upland area of Dartmoor, one of our National Parks. For the most part the central area consists of wild moorland with rocky tors and bog. It is famous

FINGLE BRIDGE, DARTMOOR

POSTBRIDGE, DARTMOOR

for its antiquities including stone crosses, circles and cromlechs of prehistoric times. Roads cross and circle the Moor, providing connection between the townships and villages: Widecombe famous for its fair; Postbridge with its clapper bridge; Lydford with old castle, gorge and waterfall; Two Bridges and Hexworthy in the very

Almshouses at Moretonhampstead

heart of the Moor, to name but a few. More visited however are the towns of the outer rim; Bovey Tracey, Chagford, Okehampton, Totnes and Ashburton, where the wooded valleys of the Teign, Tavy, Plym and Dart are of considerable beauty. Beside the River Dart near Buckfastleigh stands Buckfast Abbey on a site where St. Petrock is believed to have founded a settlement in the sixth century. The present fine Abbey Church and monastic buildings

THE BOWERMAN'S NOSE, DARTMOOR

constructed by Benedictine monks with their own hands, were completed in 1938.

Dawlish is a quiet coastal resort a little west of the Exe where the railway must be crossed to get to the sands, red like the nearby cliffs. The tranquil Dawlish Water, bordered by the flower beds and bowling green of the Lawn and the Manor Grounds Park, flows gently through the town to the sea. North-eastward the beach and sea-wall extend to Langstone Cliffs beyond which is the Warren, a long sand bar reaching out into the mouth of the River Exe. South-westward is Coryton Cove and the peculiar rock formation known as the Parson and Clerk. Popular excursions are to Mamhead House where there are lovely grounds, and to Powderham Castle, medieval seat of the Earls of Devon in a great deer park. Teignmouth stands at the mouth of the broad, sandy estuary of the Teign. There is a fine promenade with a miniature lighthouse. A long road bridge and a ferry cross the river to Shaldon where the prominent Ness Headland commands extensive views along the coast.

On the Coast near Torquay

The fine resort of Torquay, Queen of the English Riviera, stands on

BABBACOMBE QUAY

COCKINGTON FORGE, TORQUAY

UNLOADING THE CATCH, BRIXHAM

EAST GATE, TOTNES

a hillside overlooking the beautiful sweep of Tor Bay. Bathing from the Torre Abbey Sands or boating and sailing from the large harbour are the undoubted orders of the day. It is an easy walk to the high Daddy Hole Plain and on down to the sands of Meadfoot Beach. Beyond is prominent Hope's Nose, with the outlying islet of Thatcher Rock, from which the breezy Bishop's Walk leads to Anstey's Cove and the neighbouring Redgate Beach, both delightful bathing spots. A little to the north, Babbacombe Down overlooks the popular sandy beaches of Babbacombe and Oddicombe which has a cliff lift. On the west side of Torquay is pretty little Cockington village with its lovely thatched cottages and quaint old smithy's forge.

The Butterwalk, Dartmouth

Three miles south of Torquay is Paignton. Like its larger neighbour the town has all the attributes of a first-class seaside resort. Flat sand, as also at nearby Preston and Goodrington, provides safe bathing. Boating and sailing are popular. In the town are exotic parks and gardens, and a well-known zoo and botanical garden. Excursions are made to Compton Castle, a fortified manor house built in 1329 and to Berry Pomeroy Castle.

DARTMOUTH AND KINGSWEAR

THE DART AT DITTISHAM

Brixham is a picturesque fishing port and resort at the southern end of Torbay. A long harbour arm provides deep water anchorage and moorings for many fishing and pleasure craft. To the east protection is given by the lofty Berry Head where there is a lighthouse and a breezy common. The nearby St. Mary's Bay and Mamsands have popular beaches.

The interesting and ancient port of Dartmouth lies on the west side of the Dart Estuary with car-ferry connection with Kingswear on the opposite bank and its long quay provides a wonderful promenade from which to enjoy the ever-changing harbour scene. There is bathing at Castle Cove and Sugary Cove. The Butterwalk is a quaint row of seventeenth century houses.

Devon Cottages, Hope Village

Dartmouth Castle and that at Kingswear were built to defend the river mouth overlooked by St. Petrox Church. Excursion boats make the beautiful trip up the wooded River Dart to Totnes, passing the pretty waterside hamlet of Dittisham *en route.* Nearby, overlooking Start Bay, is the attractive and secluded little beach of Blackpool Sands.

Salcombe is a popular sailing and fishing resort in a magnificent position near the mouth of the Kingsbridge Estuary. There is

BOLT HEAD, SALCOMBE

THE ESTUARY, KINGSBRIDGE

THURLSTONE VILLAGE

PLYMOUTH FROM MOUNT EDGCUMBE

bathing at North and South Sands and boating trips to many other little sandy coves on the farther shore. At the head of the Salcombe inlet is the little market town of Kingsbridge. Of interest are the Shambles with quaint overhanging arcades and a pleasant quayside. Kingsbridge is the centre of the prosperous agricultural district known as the South Hams. It is bounded by a winding coastline of splendid cliff scenery and delightful coves extending from Slapton to Bolt Head, and past Bolt Tail to Thurlestone and Bigbury on the River Avon. At Hope Cove, overlooked by Bolt Tail, is a fascinating little fishing village with rocks and good bathing sands. Nearby is Thurlestone, well-known for its golf course and Bigbury-on-Sea, a little resort with Burgh Island reached by its famous tractor ferry, just offshore.

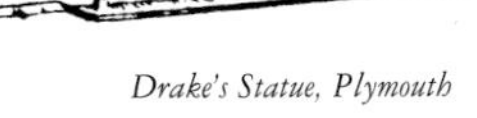

Drake's Statue, Plymouth

Plymouth is an historic old seaport with the naval dockyard of Devonport adjoining. A splendid civic and shopping centre was built after the Second World War to replace the terrible bomb damage suffered by the city. On the Hoe, with glorious views across Plymouth Sound, Drake played his famous game of bowls. His statue stands here as also does Smeaton's fine old Eddystone Lighthouse and the 17th century Royal Citadel. Parts of the old city remain around Sutton Harbour; on the Barbican a stone commemorates the departure of the Pilgrim Fathers in the "Mayflower" in 1620.

SHELLEY'S COTTAGE, LYNMOUTH

Bideford Bridge

NORTH DEVON

The beauty and elevation of the North Devon coast is characterised by high and thickly wooded cliffs. Clovelly is a picturesque village of flower-decked cottages far-famed for its one steep street which descends the 400-foot cliffside in slopes and steps to the rocky shore and tiny quay below. Along the top of the cliffs the Hobby Drive winds through thickly wooded combes for three miles to the east. Also eastwards is Bucks Mills clinging to the cliff face but here the shore below is sandy.

Bideford is a pleasant little market town and port with a famous old bridge across the River Torridge, a river popular for boating. Down at the estuary past Northam is Appledore, a quiet fishing and sailing village. Westward are the great sand flats of Northam Burrows. On the seaward side a great Pebble Ridge of smooth oval stones stretches for two miles to Westward Ho! bordered by magnificent sands, unsurpassed for surfing and sand-yachting.

The Torridge shares its estuary with the Taw on which stands the

HIGH STREET, CLOVELLY

CLOVELLY FROM THE HOBBY DRIVE

APPLEDORE FROM INSTOW

WESTWARD HO! FROM KIPLING TOR

THE SQUARE, BARNSTAPLE

fine old market town of Barnstaple, a splendid centre for North Devon tours. Of interest are the Long Bridge built in 1350, St. Ann's Chapel (1330) and the Penrose Almshouses (1659). North of the estuary is Braunton, town size but still designated village, close to Braunton Burrows now a National Nature Reserve noted for wild flowers and sea birds. A perfect expanse of flat sand stretches for three miles from the Taw estuary to Saunton Down. A golf course is attached to the hotel here but most people come for the grand bathing and surfing.

Cottages at Croyde

The wide golden bay between Saunton Down and Baggy Point is backed by high marram-covered dunes. When the tide is right the surf is magnificent. At other times many little rock pools are left to delight the youngsters. Beyond Baggy Point is the larger Morte Bay comprising Putsborough Beach and the extensive sands of Woolacombe, a popular resort; Barricane Beach at the northern end is noted for its shells.

Ilfracombe is a popular North Devon resort with shingly beach and small harbour from which boating and fishing trips may be

LANTERN HILL, ILFRACOMBE

ILFRACOMBE FROM HILLSBOROUGH

taken. Jutting into the sea is the Capstone, a huge rock around which a parade has been built. Lantern Hill stands near the harbour; on the top an old chapel now serves as a lighthouse. To the west of the town are the beautiful Torrs Walks with fine coast views to Lee Bay. Eastwards a coast road winds attractively past Watermouth to Combe Martin, a popular little resort with a rock and sand shore

Combe Martin

and a stream trickling seaward. The village proper straggles inland along a mile-long street. Favourite walks are to Great and Little Hangman hills with grand views and sandy bays at their feet. Longer excursions are to famous Hunter's Inn in a beautiful setting near Heddon's Mouth, and charming little Woody Bay.

Beautifully set amid glorious scenery are the twin villages of

CASTLE ROCK, LYNTON

MARS HILL, LYNMOUTH

Lynton and Lynmouth. Lynton sits on the wooded hilltop with a cliff lift dropping steeply to Lynmouth below, at the mouth of the tumbling Lyn rivers. Here the tiny harbour is overlooked by the picturesque cottages on Mars Hill. Grand walks are to Summerhouse Hill, the Valley of Rocks with the Castle Rock and Devil's Cheesewring, and to Lee Abbey. Favourite though is the two-and-a-half mile walk by the East Lyn river to Watersmeet, in

Lynmouth from Lynton

an exquisite setting where the Combe Park Water comes rushing to join the Lyn.

South and east of Lynmouth across the Somerset border at County Gate, lies Exmoor, a vast region of wild moorland, some 260 square miles of it designated a National Park; here the shaggy Exmoor ponies and the wild red deer roam at will the heathered slopes and sunken combes.

BY WATERSMEET, LYNMOUTH